SUPERIOR ANIMAL SENSES

HOW SNAKES AND OTHER ANIMALS TASTE THE AIR

Kristen Rajczak

PowerKiDS press

New York

Published in 2016 by The Rosen Publishing Group, Inc.
29 East 21st Street, New York, NY 10010

Copyright © 2016 by The Rosen Publishing Group, Inc.

All rights reserved. No part of this book may be reproduced in any form without permission in writing from the publisher, except by a reviewer.

First Edition

Editor: Katie Kawa
Book Design: Reann Nye

Photo Credits: Cover Asia Images/Getty Images; pp. 5, 11, 22 (teeth) reptiles4all/Shutterstock.com; p. 7 Carrie's Camera/Shutterstock.com; p. 9 EcoPrint/Shutterstock.com; p. 10 Dorling Kindersley/Getty Images; pp. 13 (top), 22 (body) John Macgregor/Photolibrary/Getty Images; pp. 13 (bottom), 22 (stretching) Sprocky/Shutterstock.com; p. 15 Sebastian Janicki/Shutterstock.com; p. 17 Ryan Ladbrook/Shutterstock.com; p. 19 (top) Paul Sutherland/National Geographic/Getty Images; p. 19 (bottom) Louise Heusinkveld/Oxford Scientific/Getty Images; p. 20 Frank Wasserfuehrer/Shutterstock.com; p. 21 PhilipYb Studio/Shutterstock.com; p. 22 (tongue, eye, ears) Reinhold Leitner/Shutterstock.com.

Library of Congress Cataloging-in-Publication Data

Rajczak, Kristen, author.
How snakes and other animals taste the air / Kristen Rajczak.
    pages cm. — (Superior animal senses)
Includes bibliographical references and index.
ISBN 978-1-4994-0995-6 (pbk.)
ISBN 978-1-4994-1033-4 (6 pack)
ISBN 978-1-4994-1079-2 (library binding)
1. Chemical senses—Juvenile literature. 2. Senses and sensation—Juvenile literature. 3. Snakes—Sense organs—Juvenile literature. 4. Jacobson's organ—Juvenile literature. 5. Pheromones—Receptors—Juvenile literature. 6. Adaptation (Biology)—Juvenile literature. I. Title.
QP455.R35 2016
573.8'77—dc23
                                    2015014998

Manufactured in the United States of America

CPSIA Compliance Information: Batch #WS15PK: For Further Information contact Rosen Publishing, New York, New York at 1-800-237-9932

CONTENTS

On the Hunt 4

Getting the Sense of Things 6

The Jacobson's Organ. 8

Tongue Tied 10

Messages to the Brain. 12

Those with a Backbone. 14

The Flehmen Response. 16

Mammals, Mates, and More 18

Saving Snake Senses 20

Glossary. 23

Index. 24

Websites 24

On the Hunt

A snake moves silently over the ground, its body curving into an S shape as it goes. Its tongue flicks in and out of its mouth. A few feet ahead, a little mouse stands in a pile of leaves. The snake starts to close in on its **prey**. No matter what direction the mouse runs, the snake follows it with ease. The snake's tongue continues to move—almost too quickly to see.

Suddenly, the snake strikes! It opens its mouth wide, and it swallows the mouse whole and alive. Without its amazing senses, the snake wouldn't be able to catch such a good meal.

That Makes Sense!

There are about 2,900 kinds of snakes on Earth, and they all "taste" the air with their tongue.

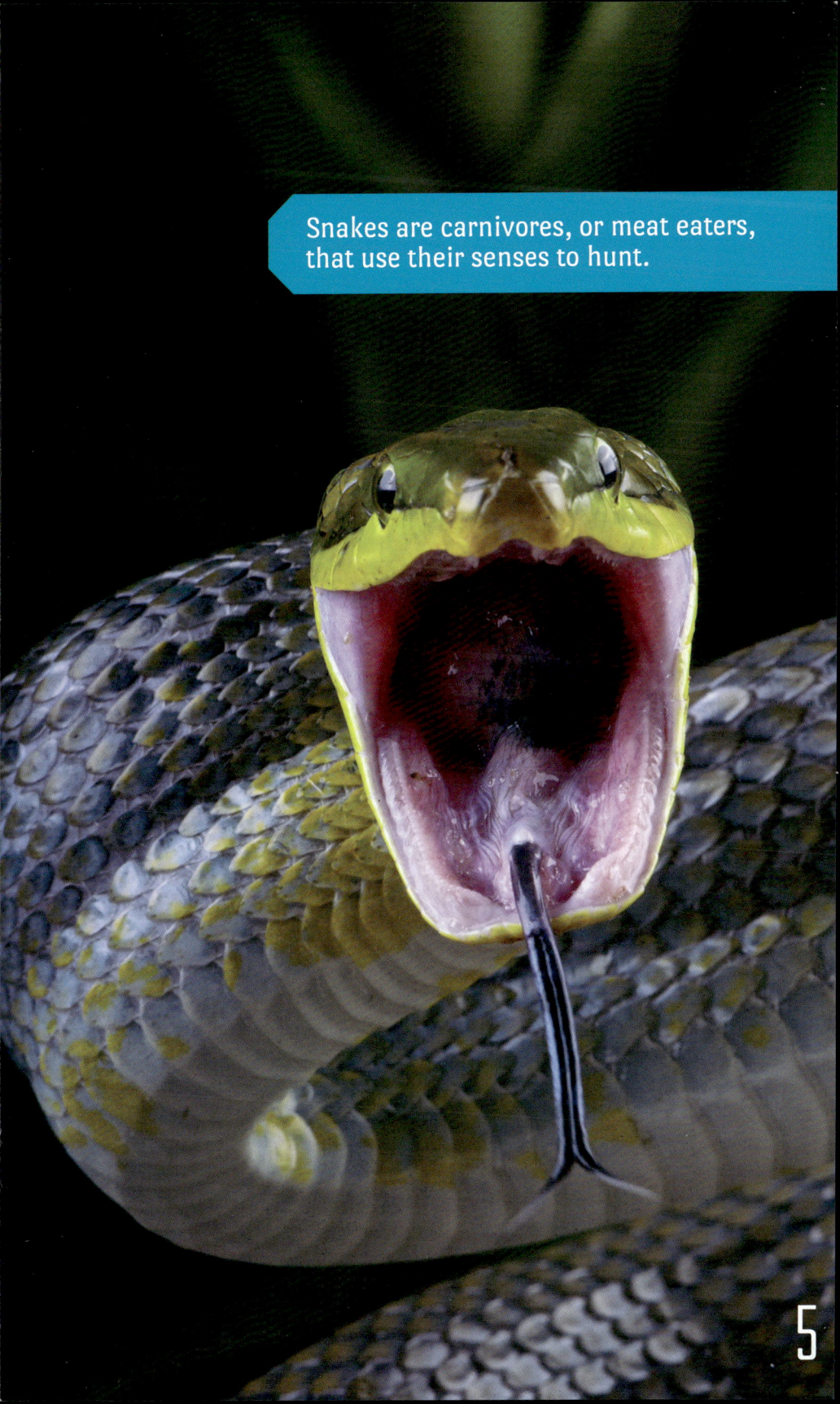

Snakes are carnivores, or meat eaters, that use their senses to hunt.

Getting the Sense of Things

Look at your nose in the mirror. The openings in your nose used to breathe and smell are called nostrils. Snakes have nostrils, too. They're even used for the same things—taking in air and sensing odors. The air snakes breathe in through their nostrils is carried to certain sensing cells where odor is **identified**.

However, snakes can only identify certain airborne smells using their nostrils. It's not their strongest way of smelling. A second olfactory, or smelling, organ senses the heavier odor **particles** carried by **moisture**. In order to use this organ, snakes have to "taste" the air with their tongue.

THAT MAKES SENSE!

An organ is a body part that does a certain job. For example, an olfactory organ's job is to sense odors.

A snake's nostrils are more important for breathing than smelling.

7

The Jacobson's Organ

The olfactory organ snakes use to smell is called the Jacobson's organ. The Jacobson's organ is also called a vomeronasal (vah-muh-roh-NAY-zuhl) organ, and it's made up of special sensing cells. In snakes, the Jacobson's organ is found on the roof of the mouth.

A snake's Jacobson's organ works along with its tongue to sense the world around it. A snake's tongue is forked, which means it splits into two parts at the end like the letter Y. Snakes seem to move their tongue in and out of their mouth almost constantly. Scientists have found that a snake moves its tongue in a certain way when it's "tasting" the air.

That Makes Sense!

The Jacobson's organ was named in the early 1800s for the Danish scientist Ludvig Levin Jacobson, who discovered the organ.

A snake's tongue is different from a person's!

Tongue Tied

Snakes aren't truly tasting the air around them like you would taste an apple or a sandwich. Their tongue flicks out of their mouth to gather odor particles. The tongue then carries these particles into the mouth and up to the Jacobson's organ. The organ has two pits in it that a snake's forked tongue fits into. The snake's tongue leaves the odor particles in these pits.

Other parts of a snake's tongue may catch odor particles, too. Once inside the snake's mouth, the particles can be pushed into its Jacobson's organ by the quick motion of its tongue.

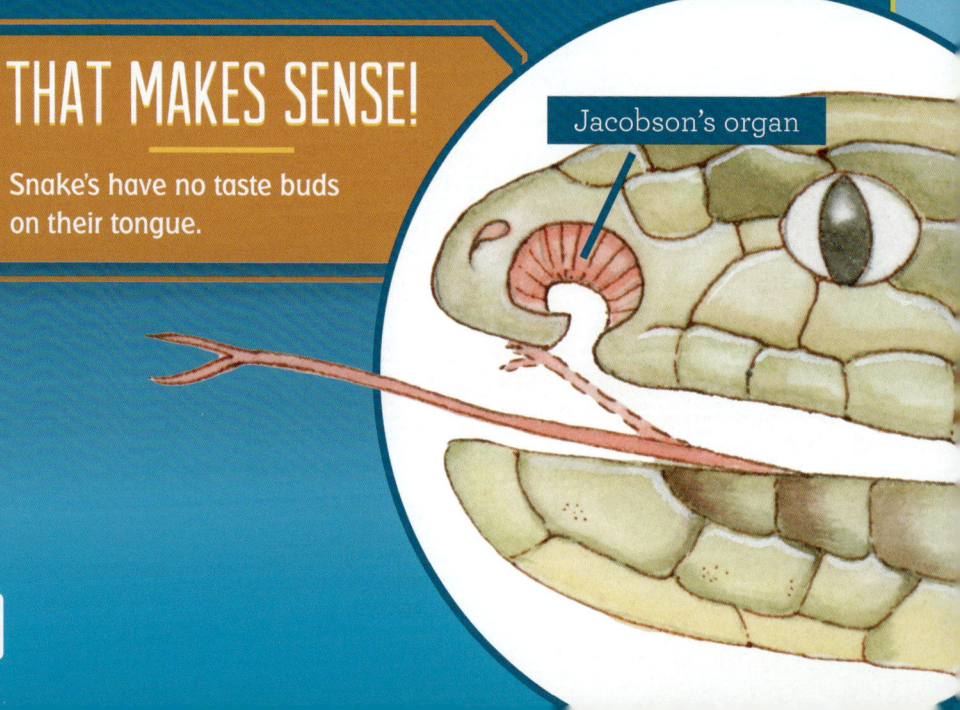

THAT MAKES SENSE!

Snake's have no taste buds on their tongue.

Jacobson's organ

Some people think the more deeply forked a snake's tongue is, the more often it uses its Jacobson's organ. It could be that those snakes just have more tongue area for sensing odors.

Messages to the Brain

Once the odor particles reach a snake's Jacobson's organ, some of the **chemicals** in them cause a message to be sent to the brain. The particles can tell the brain a lot.

Snakes mainly use their Jacobson's organ when looking for prey. It helps them identify what kind of prey is nearby. Snakes know if they're hunting a rabbit or a mouse based on the chemical message the odor particles send to their brain. The odor particles picked up on the snake's tongue can tell where the prey is, too. A snake's Jacobson's organ is a helpful hunting tool.

That Makes Sense!

Snakes hunt many different kinds of prey. Many of their body parts can **stretch** in order for the snake to eat whole animals, such as frogs and birds.

Some snakes squeeze their prey until they stop breathing. These snakes are called constrictors. Other snakes kill with their sharp teeth and venom, or poison made in their body.

Those with a Backbone

Snakes are the animals best known for "tasting" the air, but they aren't the only ones who do it. Some other reptiles also use their tongue to catch odor particles and bring them to the Jacobson's organ on the top of their mouth. Lizards, such as Gila monsters and geckos, are other reptiles that "taste" the air.

In fact, all animals that have a backbone have the chance to **develop** a vomeronasal organ, including turtles, birds, **mammals**, and many others. The organ often isn't fully formed, and sometimes it doesn't develop at all.

THAT MAKES SENSE!

People have a backbone. A vomeronasal organ starts to develop in unborn babies, but doesn't ever form fully in people.

Reptiles are cold-blooded animals covered with scales or plates that breathe air, have a backbone, and lay eggs. This gecko is a reptile that can use its tongue and Jacobson's organ to track prey.

15

The Flehmen Response

Like people, many mammals don't develop a vomeronasal organ. Others, such as cats, do. The organ is used differently than a snake's. Instead of using the tongue, mammals with a vomeronasal organ lift their top lip as if **sneering** when they take a breath. This **exposes** the Jacobson's organ to the air, so the animal can start sensing. When a mammal does this, it's called the flehmen (FLAY-muhn) response.

In mammals, the Jacobson's organ is often found in the front of the mouth. It's commonly connected to the roof of the animal's mouth, which is where a snake's Jacobson's organ is located.

That Makes Sense!

Dogs are also believed to use their Jacobson's organ to add to their strong sense of smell.

The flehmen response is easy to see in horses, as shown here.

Mammals, Mates, and More

Mammals use their Jacobson's organ to bring in odor particles and gather chemical **information** that the organ sends to the brain. Male mammals might expose their Jacobson's organ around a female to see if she's ready to find a **mate**. They might also do this when they sense a new smell. Cats use their Jacobson's organ to identify the smell of another cat that's been in the area. Scientists don't yet know all the reasons mammals use this sense organ.

Elephants also use a vomeronasal organ to learn more about the world around them, but they don't lift their lip to do so like other mammals. They use the tip of their trunk.

THAT MAKES SENSE!

When animals are ready to find a mate, they give off chemicals called pheromones, which send messages to other animals of the same species, or kind. The Jacobson's organ is used to sense these pheromones.

Lions are one mammal that use the flehmen response when finding a mate. They use it to sense the pheromones of other lions.

Saving Snake Senses

Global climate change is the warming of Earth's average **temperature**. It's caused by harmful gases that are created by the burning of many kinds of fuel, including gas used in cars and trucks. Snakes' and other reptiles' body temperature depends on the air around them. If Earth warms up too much, their bodies may stop working properly. This could affect their senses, including their ability to "taste" the air.

Snakes depend on their superior senses every day as they live and hunt. A snake's ability to "taste" the air is just one of the many reasons why these animals are such feared hunters.

That Makes Sense!

Global climate change is causing Earth's seas to rise. This could be harmful to many snakes and lizards, including the marine lizard.

Snakes, lizards, and other animals could face many problems if Earth's temperature continues to rise.

THE AMAZING SNAKE

body of some snakes can squeeze prey to death

inner ear gathers sound from vibrations, or small movements caused by sound waves

mouth and stomach can stretch to fit in large prey

sharp teeth can hold prey and sometimes poison them

tongue gathers odor particles from air and carries them to the Jacobson's organ to be identified

some snakes have great eyesight

GLOSSARY

chemical: Matter that can be mixed with other matter to cause changes.

develop: To grow over time.

expose: To show or open to the air.

identify: To find out or show what something is.

information: Knowledge or facts about something.

mammal: Any warm-blooded animal whose babies drink milk and whose body is covered with hair or fur.

mate: One of two living things that come together to produce babies.

moisture: A small amount of a liquid that makes something wet.

particle: A very small piece of matter.

prey: An animal hunted by other animals for food.

sneer: An expression that looks like a smile and is often used to show dislike or anger.

stretch: To pull tightly.

temperature: How hot or cold something is.

INDEX

C
carnivores, 5
cats, 16, 18
chemicals, 12, 18
climate change, 20
constrictors, 13

D
dogs, 16

E
elephants, 18

F
flehmen response, 16, 17, 19

G
geckos, 14, 15
Gila monsters, 14

H
horses, 17

J
Jacobson, Ludvig Levin, 8
Jacobson's organ, 8, 10, 11, 12, 14, 15, 16, 18, 22

L
lions, 19
lip, 16, 18

M
mammals, 14, 16, 18, 19
mouth, 4, 8, 10, 14, 16, 22

N
nostrils, 6, 7

O
odor particles, 6, 10, 12, 14, 18, 22
olfactory organ, 6, 8

P
pheromones, 18, 19
prey, 4, 12, 13, 15, 22

R
reptiles, 14, 15, 20

T
tongue, 4, 6, 8, 9, 10, 11, 12, 14, 15, 16, 22

V
vomeronasal organ, 8, 14, 16, 18

WEBSITES

Due to the changing nature of Internet links, PowerKids Press has developed an online list of websites related to the subject of this book. This site is updated regularly. Please use this link to access the list: www.powerkidslinks.com/sas/snake